I. W. W. SONGS

CW00740178

TO FAN THE

A Reprint of the
Nineteenth Edition (1923)
of the famous
"Little Red Song Book"

PM Press
2014

JOE HILL

INDEX

THE REBEL GIRL

Words and Music by Joe Hill

There are women of many descriptions
   In this queer world, as everyone knows,
Some are living in beautiful mansions,
   And are wearing the finest of clothes.
There are blue blooded queens and princesses,
   Who have charms made of diamonds and pearl;
But the only and thoroughbred lady
   Is the Rebel Girl.

CHORUS

**That's the Rebel Girl, that's the Rebel Girl!
To the working class she's a precious pearl.
She brings courage, pride and joy
To the fighting Rebel Boy.
We've had girls before, but we need some more
In the Industrial Workers of the World.
For it's great to fight for freedom
With a Rebel Girl.**

Yes, her hands may be hardened from labor,
   And her dress may not be very fine;
But a heart in her bosom is beating
   That is true to her class and her kind.
And the grafters in terror are trembling
   When her spite and defiance she'll hurl;
For the only and thoroughbred lady
   Is the Rebel Girl.

Words and Music of "The Rebel Girl" may be obtained
in popular sheet form by applying to I. W. W. Publishing
Bureau.   Price 25 cents.

THE INTERNATIONALE
By Eugene Pottier
(Translated by Charles H. Kerr)

Arise, ye prisoners of starvation!
  Arise, ye wretched of the earth,
For justice thunders condemnation,
  A better world's in birth.
No more tradition's chains shall bind us,
  Arise, ye slaves; no more in thrall!
The earth shall rise on new foundations,
  We have been naught, we shall be all.

REFRAIN
  'Tis the final conflict,
    Let each stand in his place,
  The Industrial Union
    Shall be the human race.

We want no condescending saviors
  To rule us from a judgment hall;
We workers ask not for their favors;
  Let us consult for all.
To make the thief disgorge his booty
  To free the spirit from its cell,
We must ourselves decide our duty,
  We must decide and do it well.

Behold them seated in their glory,
  The kings of mine and rail and soil!
What have you read in all their story,
  But how they plundered toil?
Fruits of the workers' toil are buried
  In the strong coffers of a few;
In working for their restitution
  The men will only ask their due.

6

WE WILL SING ONE SONG

By Joe Hill

(Air: "My Old Kentucky Home")

We will sing one song of the meek and humble slave,
  The horny-handed son of toil,
He's toiling hard from the cradle to the grave,
  But his master reaps the profit from his toil.
Then we'll sing one song of the greedy master class,
  They're vagrants in broadcloth, indeed,
They live by robbing the ever-toiling mass,
  Human blood they spill to satisfy their greed.

Chorus

Organize! Oh, toilers, come organize your might;
Then we'll sing one song of the workers' commonwealth.
Full of beauty, full of love and health.

We will sing one song of the politician sly,
  He's talking of changing the laws;
Election day all the drinks and smokes he'll buy,
  While we make the welkin ring with our applause.
Then we'll sing one song of the girl below the line,
  She's scorned and despised everywhere,
While in their mansions the "keepers" wine and dine
  From the profits that immoral traffic bear.

We will sing one song of the preacher, fat and sleek,
  He tells you of homes in the sky.
He says, "Be generous, be lowly and meek,
  If you don't you'll sure get roasted when you die."
Then we'll sing one song of the poor and ragged tramp,
  He carries his home on his back;
Too old to work, he's not wanted 'round the camp,
  So he wanders without aim along the track.

We will sing one song of the children in the mills,
  They're taken from playgrounds and schools,
In tender years made to go the pace that kills,
  In the sweatshops, 'mong the looms and the spools.
Then we'll sing one song of the One Big Union Grand,
  The hope of the toiler and slave,
It's coming fast! it is sweeping sea and land,
  To the terror of the grafter and the knave.

WORKERS OF THE WORLD, AWAKEN!

By Joe Hill

Workers of the world, awaken!
  Break your chains, demand your rights.
All the wealth you make is taken
  By exploiting parasites.
Shall you kneel in deep submission
  From your cradles to your graves?
Is the height of your ambition
  To be good and willing slaves?

Chorus

Arise, ye prisoners of starvation!
Fight for your own emancipation;
Arise, ye slaves of every nation.
      In One Union grand.
Our little ones for bread are crying,
And millions are from hunger dying;
The end the means is justifying,
      'Tis the final stand.

If the workers take a notion,
    They can stop all speeding trains;
Every ship upon the ocean
    They can tie with mighty chains
Every wheel in the creation,
    Every mine and every mill,
Fleets and armies of the nation,
    Will at their command stand still.

Join the union, fellow workers,
    Men and women, side by side;
We will crush the greedy shirkers
    Like a sweeping, surging tide;
For united we are standing,
    But divided we will fall;
Let this be our understanding—
    "All for one and one for all."

Workers of the world, awaken!
    Rise in all your splendid might;
Take the wealth that you are making,
    It belongs to you by right.

No one will for bread be crying,
    We'll have freedom, love and health.
When the grand red flag is flying
    In the Workers' Commonwealth.

———

A shorter workday for all employed workers would put thousands of unemployed to work. If everybody worked there would be no poverty.

CHORUS

It's a union for true Liberty
It's a union for you and for me;
It's the workers' own choice,
It's for girls and for boys,
Who want freedom from wage slavery;
And we march with a Red Flag ahead,
'Cause the blood of all nations is red—
Come on and join in the fray,
Come on and join us today,
We are fighting for Freedom and Bread.

The master's class in fear have kept us shaking,
　For long in bondage they held us fast;
But the fight the Industrial Workers are now making
　Will make our chains a relic of the past.
Industrial unionism now is calling,
　The toilers of the world they hear its cry;
In line with the Industrial Workers they are falling,
　By their principles to stand or fall and die.

HARVEST WAR SONG

By Pat Brennan

(Tune: "Tipperary")

We are coming home, John Farmer; we are coming back
　　to stay.
For nigh on fifty years or more, we've gathered up your
　　hay.
We have slept out in your hayfields, we have heard your
　　morning shout;
We've heard you wondering where in hell's them pesky
　　go-abouts?

12

CHORUS

It's a long way, now understand me; it's a long way to
      town;
It's a long way across the prairie, and to hell with
      Farmer John.
Here goes for better wages, and the hours must come
      down;
For we're out for a winter's stake this summer, and we
      want no scabs around.

You've paid the going wages, that's what kept us on
      the bum.
You say you've done your duty, you chin-whiskered son
      of a gun.
We have sent your kids to college, but still you rave
      and shout.
And call us tramps and hoboes, and pesky go-abouts.

But now the long wintry breezes are a-shaking our poor
      frames,
And the long drawn days of hunger try to drive us boes
      insane.
It is driving us to action—we are organized today;
Us pesky tramps and hoboes are coming back to stay.

YOU cannot be free while your CLASS is enslave

Join the I. W. W. and find YOUR place in the final battle

for the emancipation of the world's workers.

DUMP THE BOSSES OFF YOUR BACK

By John Brill

(Tune: "Take It to the Lord in Prayer")

Are you poor, forlorn and hungry?
　Are there lots of things you lack?
Is your life made up of misery?
　Then dump the bosses off your back.
Are your clothes all patched and tattered?
　Are you living in a shack?
Would you have your troubles scattered?
　Then dump the bosses off your back.

Are you almost split asunder?
　Loaded like a long-eared jack?
Boob—why don't you buck like thunder?
　And dump the bosses off your back?
All the agonies you suffer,
　You can end with one good whack—
Stiffen up, you orn'ry duffer—
　And dump the bosses off your back.

ALL HELL CAN'T STOP US!

(Tune: "Hold the Fort")

(Written by Ralph H. Chaplin, in Leavenworth Pen.)

Now the final battle rages;
　Tyrants quake with fear.
Rulers of the New Dark Ages
　Know THEIR end is near.

CHORUS
Scorn to take the crumbs they drop us;
All is ours by right!
Onward, men! All Hell can't stop us!
Crush the Parasite!

With a world-wide revolution
  Bring them to your feet!
They of crime and persecution—
  They must work to eat!

Tear the mask of lies asunder;
  Let the truth be known;
With a voice of angry thunder,
  Rise and claim your own!

Down with Greed and Exploitation;
  Tyranny must fall!
Hail to Toil's Emancipation;
  Labor shall be all.

UP FROM YOUR KNEES

By Ralph H. Chaplin
(Air: "Song of a Thousand Years")

Up from your knees, ye cringing serfmen!
  What have ye gained by whines and tears?
Rise! they can never break our spirits
  Though they should try a thousand years.

CHORUS
A thousand years, then speed the victory!
Nothing can stop us nor dismay.
After the winter comes the springtime;
After the darkness comes the day.

Break ye your chains; strike off your fetters;
   Beat them to swords—the foe appears—
Slaves of the world, arise and crush him;
   Crush him or serve a thousand years.

Join in the fight—the Final Battle.
   Welcome the fray with ringing cheers.
These are the times all freemen dreamed of—
   Fought to attain a thousand years.

Be ye prepared; be not unworthy, —
   Greater the task when triumph nears.
Master the earth, O Men of Labor,—
   Long have ye learned—a thousand years.

Over the hills the sun is rising.
   Out of the gloom the light appears.
See! at your feet the world is waiting,—
   Bought with your blood a thousand years.

THE TRAMP

By Joe Hill

Tune: "Tramp, Tramp, Tramp, the Boys Are Marching."

If you all will shut your trap,
I will tell you 'bout a chap,
That was broke and up against it too, for fair;
He was not the kind to shirk,
He was looking hard for work,
But he heard the same old story everywhere.

CHORUS

Tramp, tramp, tramp, keep on a-tramping,
Nothing doing here for you;
If I catch you 'round again,
You will wear the ball and chain,
Keep on tramping, that's the best thing you can do.

He walked up and down the street,
Till the shoes fell off his feet.
In a house he spied a lady cooking stew,
And he said, "How do you do,
May I chop some wood for you?"
What the lady told him made him feel so blue.

'Cross the street a sign he read,
"Work for Jesus" so it said,
And he said, "Here is my chance, I'll surely try,"
And he kneeled upon the floor,
Till his knees got rather sore,
But at eating-time he heard the preacher cry—

Down the street he met a cop,
And the copper made him stop,
And he asked him, "When did you blow into town?
Come with me up to the judge,"
But the judge he said, "Oh fudge,
Bums that have no money needn't come around."

Finally came that happy day
When his life did pass away,
He was sure he'd go to heaven when he died,
When he reached the pearly gate,
Santa Peter, mean old skate,
Slammed the gate right in his face and loudly cried:

WHADDA YA WANT TO BREAK YOUR BACK FOR THE BOSS FOR?

(Tune: "What Do You Want to Make Those Eyes at Me For?")

Toiling along in light from morn 'til night,
Wearin' away your all for the Parasite;
Workin' like a mule with a number two,
Puffin' like a bellow when the day is through;
Steering a load of gravel through the muck and slop
Packing a hod o' mustard 'til you damn near flop;
Trying to bust a gut for two twenty-five,
Pluggin' like a sucker 'til five.

CHORUS

So whadda ya want to break your back for the boss for,
When it don't mean life to you?
Do you think it right to struggle day and night,
And plow like Hell for the Parasite?
So whadda ya want to break your back for the boss for,
When there's more in life for you?
Slow up Bill! that's the way to beat the System;
Join the Wobbly Gang, they've got the bosses guessing.
So whadda ya want to break your back for the boss for,
When it don't mean life to you?

Do it all today and you'll soon find out,
Tomorrow there'll be nothing but to hang about,
Looking at the "job sign," wondering why you rave,
With a wrinkle on your belly like an ocean wave;
Doughnuts then begin to hang a little high,
You're pinched by the Bull for a "German spy";
You're nothing but a bum, says the Judge with a smile,
Thirty days on the Rock pile.

THE WHITE SLAVE

By Joe Hill

(Air: "Meet Me Tonight in Dreamland")

One little girl, fair as a pearl,
Worked every day in a laundry;
All that she made, for food she paid,
So she slept on a park bench so soundly;
An old procuress spied her there,
She came and whispered in her ear:

CHORUS

**Come with me now, my girly,
Don't sleep out in the cold;
Your face and tresses curly
Will bring you fame and gold,
Automobiles to ride in, diamonds and silk to wear,
You'll be a star bright, down in the red light,
You'll make your fortune there.**

Same little girl, no more a pearl,
Walks all alone 'long the river,
Five years have flown, her health is gone,
She would look at the water and shiver,
Whene'er she'd stop to rest and sleep,
She'd hear a voice call from the deep:

Girls in this way, fall every day,
And have been falling for ages,
Who is to blame? You know his name,
It's the boss that pays starvation wages.
A homeless girl can always hear
Temptations calling everywhere.

THE BIG QUESTION

(Air: "America")

By T-B-S.

My Job—now is no more
   The boss has slam'd the door;
What shall I do?
   Seem's like my end is near,
My guts feel awful queer—
   Where do we go from here?
—This is up to you.

No, I've not lost a leg,
   —Why must I starve and beg?
What Shall I Do?
   Where can the answer lurk?
Why am I out of work,
   Gazing on all this murk?
This is up to you.

I can not stand alone,
   Masters have laid me prone;
What Shall I Do?
   Why can't we hand in hand,
Reclaim our right to stand,
   Unhorse the sleek brigand?
This is up to you.

Dedicated to the Open Shop drive, 1921.

The workers can never be free until they blow the whistle for the parasites to go to work.

24

SOLIDARITY FOREVER!

By Ralph H. Chaplin

(Tune: "John Brown's Body")

When the Union's inspiration through the worker's blood
    shall run,
There can be no power greater anywhere beneath the sun.
Yet what force on earth is weaker than the feeble strength
    of one?
        But the Union makes us strong.

CHORUS

Solidarity forever!
Solidarity forever!
Solidarity forever!
But the Union makes us strong.

Is there aught we hold in common with the greedy para-
    site
Who would lash us into serfdom and would crush us
    with his might?
Is there anything left for us but to organize and fight?
    For the Union makes us strong.

It is we who plowed the prairies; built the cities where
    they trade.
Dug the mines and built the workshops; endless miles of
    railroad laid.
Now we stand, outcast and starving, 'mid the wonders we
    have made;
        But the Union makes us strong.

All the world that's owned by idle drones, is ours and ours
    alone.
We have laid the wide foundations; built it skywards,
    stone by stone.

It is ours, not to slave in, but to master and to own,
      While the Union makes us strong.

They have taken untold millions that they never toiled to
    earn.
But without our brain and muscle not a single wheel can
    turn.
We can break their haughty power; gain our freedom
    when we learn
        That the Union makes us strong.

In our hands is placed a power greater than their hoarded
    gold;
Greater than the might of armies, magnified a thousand
    fold.
We can bring to birth the new world from the ashes of
    the old,
        For the Union makes us strong.

THE DOLLAR ALARM CLOCK

By John Healy

(Air: "Old Oaken Bucket")

How dear to my heart are those chimes in the morning,
That yank me from bed with melodious thrill;
How sweet is the sound of the regular warning
That yells that it's time that I hike to the mill.
Without it I'd sleep till the sun had arisen
Be late to the job that my boss le s me use;
Get canned, perhaps steal, maybe land in a prison
If the chimes didn't hustle me out of my snooze.

CHORUS

> The faithful alarm clock
> The rattling alarm clock;
> The dollar alarm clock
> That rests on my shelf.

What a blessing it was when the thing was invented
It beats the slave-driver who came with his stick;
It rests on the shelf in the shack that I rented
It never gets hungry; it never gets sick.
If overly weary I take a tin bucket
And place the alarm clock down into the thing,
When it chimes in the morning it doubles the racket;
It would wake up the dead when the two of them ring.

Sometimes the good woman gets worn out and weary
And says we are hauling too much of a load,
I tell her the journey would look still more dreary
If the dollar alarm clock should fail to explode.
Then here's to my booster that only needs winding,
And here's to the victim that just keeps alive.
The boss gets the money and I do the grinding;
The clock starts the circus at quarter past five.

———————

The present is distinctively an industrial epoch in world history. There can be no democracy in a world ruled by industrial despots. The I. W. W. stands for the only REAL democracy—Industrial Democracy.

One worker on the job is worth a dozen in the jungles.

WE HAVE FED YOU ALL FOR A THOUSAND YEARS

Poem—By an Unknown Proletarian.

Music—By Rudolph von Liebich, of the General Recruiting Union, Chicago, and Composer of Music for the Working Class.

We have fed you all, for a thousand years
And you hail us still unfed,
Though there's never a dollar of all your wealth
But marks the worker's dead.
We have yielded our best to give you rest
And you lie on crimson wool.
Then if blood be the price of all your wealth,
Good God! We have paid it in full.

There is never a mine blown skyward now
But we're buried alive for you.
There's never a wreck drifts shoreward now
But we are its ghastly crew.
Go reckon our dead by the forges red
And the factories where we spin.
If blood be the price of your cursed wealth
Good God! We have paid it in.

We have fed you all for a thousand years—
For that was our doom, you know,
From the days when you chained us in your fields
To the strike of a week ago.
You have taken our lives, and our babies and wives,
And we're told it's your legal share;
But if blood be the price of your lawful wealth
Good God! We have bought it fair.

I'M TOO OLD TO BE A SCAB

(Air: "Just Before the Battle, Mother")

By T-B-S.

Good-bye, master, I must leave you,
Something tells me I must go,
For you know I can't deceive you,
Going wage is too darn low.
Yes, you say that you will feed me
If I chop that hardwood cord;
—Do not to temptation lead me,
I'm not toiling for my board.

Though my trials have been sundry,
I must e'er disdain to moan
And although I'm awful hungry,
I would leave "your work" alone.
Yes, I fear I cannot tarry—
And I know just how you feel
But you see, if I'm to marry
I must earn a double meal.

If I work for bread and lodging
While the sun is high and warm;
It would cause me sundry dodging
Through the winter's cold and storm.
I must have the all that's in it—
In the labor that I sell;
For you cannot tell what minute
It may start to rain like hell.

One more question, boss, one only—
As you count your wealth untold
Would you have me save bologny—
'Gainst the day when I am old?
Now we understand each other
(As we play the game of grab)
But, please do recall, "my brother"
I'm too old to be a scab.

MR. BLOCK

By Joe Hill
(Air: "It Looks to Me Like a Big Time Tonight")

Please give me your attention, I'll introduce to you
A man that is a credit to "Our Red, White and Blue";
His head is made of lumber, and solid as a rock;
He is a common worker and his name is Mr. Block.
And Block he thinks he may
Be President some day.

CHORUS

Oh, Mr. Block, you were born by mistake,
You take the cake,
You make me ache.
Tie on a rock to your block and then jump in the lake,
Kindly do that for Liberty's sake.

Yes, Mr. Block is lucky; he found a job, by gee!
The sharks got seven dollars, for job and fare and fee.
They shipped him to a desert and dumped him with his
truck,
But when he tried to find his job, he sure was out of luck.
He shouted, "That's too raw,
I'll fix them with the law."

Block hiked back to the city, but wasn't doing well.
He said, I'll join the union—the great A. F. of L."
He got a job next morning, got fired in the night,
He said, "I'll see Sam Gompers and he'll fix that foreman
      right."
Sam Gompers said, "You see,
You've got our sympathy."

Election day he shouted, "A Socialist for Mayor!"
The "comrade" got elected, he happy was for fair,
But after the election he got an awful shock.
A great big socialistic Bull did rap him on the block.
And Comrade Block did sob,
"I helped him to his job."

Poor Block, he died one evening, I'm very glad to state;
He climbed the golden ladder up to the pearly gate.
He said, "Oh, Mr. Peter, one word I'd like to tell,
I'd like to meet the Astorbilts and John D. Rockefell."
Old Pete said, "Is that so?
You'll meet them down below."

THE INDUSTRIAL WORKERS OF THE WORLD

By Laura Payne Emerson.
(Air: Wabash Cannonball)

I stood by a city prison,
In the twilight's deepening gloom,
Where men and women languished
In a loathsome, living tomb.
They were singing! And their voices
Seemed to weave a wreath of light,
As the words came clear with meaning:
"Workers of the World, unite!"

As it was with Galileo,
And all thinkers of the past,
So with these Industrial Workers,
Tyrants' shackles hold them fast.
In the bastiles of the nations,
They are bludgeoned, mugged and starved,
While upon their aching bodies
Prints of whips and clubs are carved.

Yet with spirits still unbroken
And with hope for future years
They are calling to their fellows:
"Come, arise! and dry your tears.
Wake, ye toilers, get in action,
Break your bonds, exert your might—
You can make this hell a heaven,
Workers of the World, unite!"

Hail! ye brave Industrial Workers,
Vanguard of the coming day,
When labor's hosts shall cease to cringe
And shall dash their chains away.
How the masters dread you, hate you,
Their uncompromising foe;
For they see in you a menace,
Threatening soon their overthrow.

———————

"Yaas," said the farmer reflectively, "all the I. W. W.
fellers I've met seem to be pretty decent lads, but them
'alleged I. W. W.'s'" must be holy frights."

THE WORKERS' MARSELLLAISE

Ye sons of toil, awake to glory!
  Hark, hark, what myriads bid you rise;
Your children, wives and grandsires hoary—
    Behold their tears and hear their cries!
    Behold their tears and hear their cries!
Shall hateful tyrants mischief breeding,
  With hireling hosts, a ruffian band—
  Affright and desolate the land,
While peace and liberty lie bleeding?

CHORUS

To arms! to arms! ye brave!
....Th' avenging sword unsheathe!
  March on, march on, all hearts resolved
    On Victory or Death.

With luxury and pride surrounded,
  The vile, insatiate despots dare,
Their thirst for gold and power unbounded
    To mete and vend the light and air,
    To mete and vend the light and air,
Like beasts of burden, would they load us,
  Like gods would bid their slaves adore,
  But man is man, and who is more?
Then shall they longer lash and goad us?

O, Liberty can man resign thee?
  Once having felt thy generous flame,
Can dungeon's bolts and bars confine thee?
  Or whips, thy noble spirit tame?
  Or whips, thy noble spirit tame?
Too long the world has wept bewailing,
  That Falsehood's dagger tyrants wield;
  But Freedom is our sword and shield;
And all their arts are unavailing!

33

"REMEMBER"

(Tune: "Hold the Fort")

We speak to you from jail today
  Two hundred union men,
We're here because the bosses' laws
  Bring slavery again.

CHORUS

In Chicago's darkened dungeons
  For the O. B. U.
Remember you're outside for us
  While we're in here for you.

We're here from mine and mill and rail
  We're here from off the sea,
From coast to coast we make the boast
  Of Solidarity.

We laugh and sing, we have no fear
  Our hearts are always light,
We know that every Wobbly true
  Will carry on the fight.

We make a pledge—no tyrant might
  Can make us bend the knee,
Come on, you worker, organize,
  And fight for Liberty..

HARRISON GEORGE
Cook County Jail, Oct. 18, 1917

———

An ounce of ORGANIZATION is worth a ton of talk; join the One Big Union and help to free yourself and your class from wage slavery.

INDUSTRIAL UNIONISM SPEAKS TO TOILERS OF THE SEA

By Harold R. Johnston

(Air: "Stung Right")

"You men who toil upon the ships—
   The ships of every sea—
Come bear to me your grievances,
   Your tales of misery;
For I am strong and good and great,
   The trusts must bow to me;
For I shall take all workers in
   And bring them victory."

CHORUS

Seamen! Come all—join the O. B. U.!
Fearless fighters, every one, and true!
For, when we are all lined up, in the industry,
Labor will be master, over the sea!

"You've weathered storms upon the deck,
   O, Toilers of the Sea;
You've fallen in the fire-holes
   In the days that used to be.
But now the times must change about,
   A New Day must appear
When all you Toilers of the Sea,
   Begin to see and hear."

"I speak to you, O Workingmen,
  O, Toilers of the Sea;
Come organize one union great —
  The shipping industry.
When you are thusly organized,
  With others like your own,
The One Big Union of the World
  Shall rule the earth, ALONE!"

THE PREACHER AND THE SLAVE

By Joe Hill

(Tune: "Sweet Bye and Bye")

Long-haired preachers come out every night,
Try to tell you what's wrong and what's right;
But when asked how 'bout something to eat
They will answer with voices so sweet:

CHORUS
You will eat, bye and bye,
In that glorious land above the sky;
Work and pray, live on hay,
You'll get pie in the sky when you die.

And the starvation army they play,
And they sing and they clap and they pray,
Till they get all your coin on the drum,
Then they tell you when you're on the bum:

Holy Rollers and Jumpers come out,
And they holler, they jump and they shout
"Give your money to Jesus," they say,
"He will cure all diseases today."

If you fight hard for children and wife—
Try to get something good in this life—
You're a sinner and bad man, they tell,
When you die you will sure go to hell.

Workingmen of all countries, unite,
Side by side we for freedom will fight:
When the world and its wealth we have gained
To the grafters we'll sing this refrain:

LAST CHORUS
You will eat, bye and bye,
When you've learned how to cook and to fry;
Chop some wood, 'twill do you good,
And you'll eat in the sweet bye and bye.

"THE POPULAR WOBBLY"

(Air: "They Go Wild, Simply Wild Over Me")

By T-Bone Slim

I'm as mild manner'd man as can be
And I've never done them harm that I can see,
Still on me they put a ban and they threw me in the can,
They go wild, simply wild over me.

They accuse me of ras—cal—i—ty
But I can't see why they always pick on me,
I'm as gentle as a lamb, but they take me for a ram,
They go wild, simply wild over me.

Oh the "bull" he went wild over me
And he held his gun where everyone could see,
He was breathing rather hard when he saw my union
        card—
He went wild, simply wild over me.

Then the judge he went wild over me
And I plainly saw we never would agree,
So I let the man obey what his conscience had to say,
He went wild, simply wild over me.

Oh the jailer went wild over me
And he locked me up and threw away the key—
It seems to be the rage so they keep me in a cage,
They go wild, simply wild over me.

They go wild, simply wild over me,
I'm referring to the bed-bug and the flea,
They disturb my slumber deep and I murmur in my sleep,
They go wild, simply wild over me.

Even God, he went wild over me,
This I found out when I knelt upon my knee,
Did he hear my humble yell? No, he told me "Go to
        hell,"
He went wild, simply wild over me.

Will the roses grow wild over me
When I'm gone to the land that is to be?
When my soul and body part in the stillness of my heart—
Will the roses grow wild over me?

"RENUNCIATION"

(Air: "Auld Lang Syne")

By Joachim Raucher

When hungry millions are unfed
    And the little orphans weep,
I cannot eat in peace my bread,
    Nor sing my grief to sleep.
When thoughts arising from the heart
    Are hampered in their flight,
I cannot sit and muse apart
    Upon a dreamy height.

When craven lies oft seek to blind
    The eyes of blazing Truth,
I cannot turn my maddened mind
    To songs of love and youth,
Nor can I sing in lyric strains
    Of private, little woes,
When Greed is reaping golden gains
    From bloody seeds it sows.

"For my part, I sympathize with them. While they are threatened and imprisoned, I am manacled. If they are denied a living wage, I, too, am defrauded. While they are industrial slaves I cannot be free. My hunger is not satisfied while they are hindered and neglected. When they are flung out on a desert under a scorching sun, I too, burn, and my soul is athirst. When one of them is dragged from his bed and hung to a railroad trestle, a great horror of darkness falls upon my spirit, and from the depths of my heart I cry out against those who persecute the weak and unfriended."—Helen Keller.

DON'T TAKE MY PAPA AWAY FROM ME

Words and Music by Joe Hill

(Written just before his execution)

A little girl with her father stayed, in a cabin across
    the sea,
Her mother dear in the cold grave lay; with her father
    she'd always be—
But then one day the great war broke out and the father
    was told to go;
The little girl pleaded—her father she needed.
    She begged, cried and pleaded so:

CHORUS

Don't take my papa away from me, don't leave me there
    all alone.
He has cared for me so tenderly, ever since mother was
    gone.
Nobody ever like him can be, no one can so with me play.
Don't take my papa away from me; please don't take
    papa away.

Her tender pleadings were all in vain, and her father
    went to the war.
He'll never kiss her good night again, for he fell 'mid the
    cannons' roar.
Greater soldier was never born, but his brave heart was
    pierced one day;
And as he was dying, he heard some one crying,
    A girl's voice far away:

40

WHEN YOU WEAR THAT BUTTON

(Tune: "When You Wore a Tulip")
By Richard Brazier

I met him in Dakota when the harvesting was o'er,
A "Wob" he was, I saw by the button that he wore.
He was talking to a bunch of slaves in the jungles near
    the tracks;
He said, "You guys whose hoes are on your backs;
Why don't you stick together with the 'Wobblies' in one
    band
And fight to change conditions for the workers in this
    land?"

CHORUS

When you wear that button, the "Wobblies" red button
  And carry their red, red card,
No need to hike, boys, along these old pikes, boys,
  Every "Wobbly" will be your pard.
The boss will be leery, the "stiffs" will be cheery
  When we hit John Farmer hard,
They'll all be affrighted, when we stand united
  And carry that Red, Red Card.

The "stiffs" all seemed delighted, when they heard him
    talk that way.
They said, "We need more pay, and a shorter working
    day."
The "Wobbly" said, "You'll get these things without the
    slightest doubt
If you'll organize to knock the bosses out.
If you'll join the One Big Union, and wear their badge of
    liberty
You'll strike the blow all slaves must strike if they would
    be free."

MY WANDERING BOY

Where is my wandering boy tonight?
The boy of his mother's pride,
He's counting the ties with his bed on his back,
Or else he is bumming a ride.

CHORUS

Oh, where is my boy tonight?
Oh, where is my boy tonight?
He's on the head end of an overland train—
That's where your boy is tonight.

II

His heart may be pure as the morning dew,
But his clothes are a sight to see.
He's pulled for a vag, his excuse won't do.
"Thirty days," says the judge, you see.

Oh, where is my boy tonight?
Oh, where is my boy tonight?
The chilly wind blows, to the lock-up he goes,
That's where your boy is tonight.

III

"I was looking for work, Oh judge," he said.
Says the judge, "I have heard that before."
So to join the chain gang far off—he is led
To hammer the rocks some more.

Oh, where is my boy tonight?
Oh, where is my boy tonight?
To strike many blows for the country he goes,
That's where your boy is tonight.

IV

Don't search for your wandering boy tonight,
Let him play the old game if he will—
A worker, or bum, he'll ne'er be right,
So long's he's a wage slave still.

Oh where is my boy tonight?
His money is "out of sight."
Wherever he "blows," up against it he goes,
Here's luck!—to your boy tonight.

THE EVERETT COUNTY JAIL

(Tune: "Tramp, Tramp, Tramp, the Boys are Marching")

By William Whalen

In the prison cell we sit
Are we broken hearted—nit.
We're as happy and as cheerful as can be,
For we know that every Wob
Will be busy on the job,
Till they swing the prison doors and set us free.

CHORUS

Are you busy, Fellow Workers,
Are your shoulders to the wheel?
Get together for the cause
And some day you'll make the laws,
It's the only way to make the masters squeal.

Though the living is not grand,
Mostly mush and "coffee and,"
It's as good as we expected when we came.
It's the way they treat the slave
In this free land of the brave,
There is no one but the working class to blame.

When McRae, and Veith, and Black
To the Lumberyards go back
May they travel empty handed as they came.
May they turn in their report
That the Wobs still hold the fort,
That a rebel is an awful thing to tame.

When the 65 per cent
That they call the "working gent"
Organizes in a Union of its class,
We will then get what we're worth
That will be the blooming earth.
Organize and help to bring the thing to pass.

I WANNA FREE MISS LIBERTY

(Air: "Sunny Tennessee")

By T-B-S.

While the moon was softly shining
On my cot, as I lay pining,
Thinking of the day—long passed away;
Came a drowsy feeling o'er me—
And Joe Hill stood there before me—
I seem'd to hear this joyous fighter say:

CHORUS

I came to free Miss Liberty, from the bonds of slavery;
From mock Democracy; from inequality;
I want to feel no Iron Heel shall disgrace our peaceful
shore;
That all the world may do away with war—
I love to dream the old, old dream, that tomorrow I will
find
Men of a kindred mind—who love their fellow kind.
I long to make this plea, say not that it cannot be,
I want to see the whole world free from the chains
of slavery.

II

Let us then be up and doing—
Greater Times and things are brewing
Oh, Organize!—The One Big Union Way:
"Workers of the world, awaken."
"All the wealth you make is taken."
"Break your chains." I hear the spirit say:

III

Tighter are the class lines drawing—
Hunger at our vitals gnawing—
My reason sways and I long to pray?
Rises then again before us
Spectres of a Martyred chorus—
I seem to hear these sterling fighters say:

———

Industrial Unionism is the royal road to Industrial
Freedom.

MAY DAY SONG

Words by Ralph Chaplin

Music by Rudolph von Liebich

O, Labor Day, O, First of May,
   Welcomed and honored on land and on sea.
Winter so drear must disappear,
   Fair days are coming for you and for me.
We, of the old world, building the New,
Ours is the will and the power to do;
   Then let us sing, hail to the Spring—
Hail to the Day we can strike to be free!

Banner so red, high overhead,
   Hated and feared by the powers that be!
In every land firmly we stand;
   Men of all nations who labor are we.
Under one banner, standing as one,
Claiming the earth and our place in the sun.
   Then let us sing, hail to the Spring—
Hail to the Day we can strike to be free!

O, Labor Day, O, First of May,
   Warm with the gleam of the bright days to be!
Join in the throng, fearless and strong—
   One mighty Union of world industry.
Shoulder to shoulder, each in his place,
Ours is the hope of the whole human race.
   Then let us sing, hail to the Spring—
Hail to the Day we can strike to be free!

THEY'LL SOON RING OUT

By John E. Nordquist

(Air: Where the Sunset Turns the Ocean's Blue to Gold)

We are looking for that time,
When the bells of earth shall chime
To proclaim a world of workers really free.
I can see that joyous day
Not so very far away
And the vision puts a hopeful heart in me.
I can see the wage slave free,
With his children by his knee,
And his darling wife is bubbling o'er with cheer;
And the childish faces smile,
Nothing can their joy defile,
For they hear the bells of freedom ringing clear.

CHORUS

Oh I hear those free bells ringing
And the toilers all are singing,
For the miseries of the past have flown away.
And a worker's world I see,
Where no misery can be;
How I long to hear those bells on Freedom's Day.

If you wish to speed those times,
If you long to hear those chimes,
Do your part in organizing all the slaves.
If we're going to see that day
You must help to clear the way;

We must end the reign of cap'talistic knaves.
    We must capture industry,
    All the ships upon the sea—
Ev'ry fact'ry, mine and mill, we're going to take.
    When the boss gets overalls,
    Then the cause of mis'ry falls
And those sleeping bells of freedom shall awake.

ONWARD, "ONE BIG UNION!"

By Ralph Cheney

(To be sung to the tune of "Onward, Christian Soldiers")

Onward, One Big Union,
Joy and justice led,
With the Free Society
Shining out ahead!
Freedom, our one master,
Leads against the foe.

REFRAIN

Gates of jails can never
'Gainst our will prevail.
We've the world's one power;
And we cannot fail.

Forward unto battle
We, the workers, go.
Onward, One Big Union,
Joy and justice led
With the free society
Shining out ahead!

War and wrong shall perish,
Poverty shall cease.
Hatred, wrath, and slavery
Yield to joy and peace.

48

COUNT YOUR WORKERS—COUNT THEM!

(Air: "Count Your Blessings")

An employment shark one day I went to see,
And he said, "Come in and buy a job from me;
Just a couple of dollars for an office fee,
But the job is steady—and the fare is free."

CHORUS

Count your pennies— count them one by one,
Then you'll plainly see how "easy you are done."
Count your pennies, take them in your hand,
Sneak into a "Jap's" and get a coffee and—

II

I shipped out—and worked—and slept in lousy bunks,
And the grub!—It stunk as bad as nineteen skunks.
When I worked a week the boss he said one day,
"You're too tired, you're fired, go and get your pay."

III

When I went to get my pay, Oh, Holy Gee!
Road and School and Poll tax—and Hospital fee,
Then I nearly fainted and I lost my sense . . .
When the clerk he said, "You owe me fifty cents."

IV

When I got back to town with blisters on my feet,
There I saw a fellow speaking on the street,
And he said, it is the workers' own mistake—
If they'd stick together they'd get all they make!

V

And he says, Who'll come and join our union grand,
Who will be the first—to join our "fighting" band?
Write me out a card, says I, right here, by gee!
The Industrial Workers is the "dope" for me!

CHORUS

Count your workers, count them one by one
Stand! we'll show the bosses how it's really done—
Stand together, Workers—Hand in Hand!
Then—you'll never have to live on coffee and—

FIFTY THOUSAND LUMBERJACKS

(Tune: "Portland County Jail")

Fifty thousand lumberjacks, fifty thousand packs,
Fifty thousand dirty rolls of blankets on their backs,
Fifty thousand minds made up to strike and strike like
         men;
For fifty years they've "packed" a bed, but never will
         again.

CHORUS

"Such a lot of devils," that's what the papers say—
They've gone on strike for shorter hours and some in-
    crease in pay.
They left the camps, the lazy tramps, they all walked out
    as one;
They say they'll win the strike or put the bosses on the
    bum."

Fifty thousand wooden bunks full of things that crawl;
Fifty thousand restless men have left them once for all.
One by one they dared not say, "Fat, the hours are long."
If they did, they'd hike—but now they're fifty thousand
strong.

Fatty Rich, we know you're game, know your pride is
pricked.
Say—but why not be a man, and own when you are
licked?
They've joined the One Big Union—Gee! For goodness
sake, "Get wise!"
The more you try to buck them now the more they organize.

Take a tip and start right in—plan some cozy rooms,
Six or eight spring beds in each, with towels, sheets and
brooms;
Shower baths for men who work keeps them well and fit.
A laundry, too, and drying room, would help a little bit.

Get some dishes, white and clean; good pure food to eat.
See that cook has help enough to keep the table neat.
Tap the bell for eight hours' work; treat the boys like
men,
And fifty thousand lumberjacks may come to work again.

Men who work should be well paid. "A man's a man for
a' that."
Many a man has a home to keep same as yourself, Old
Fat.
Mothers, sisters, sweethearts, wives, children, too, galore,
Stand behind the men to win this bread and butter war.

TIE 'EM UP!

Words and Music by G. G. Allen

I

We have no fight with brothers of the old A. F. of L.
But we ask you to use your reason with the facts we
 have to tell.
Your craft is but protection for a form of property,
The skill that you are losing, don't you see.
Improvements on machinery take your tool and skill
 away,
And you'll be among the common slaves upon some fateful
 day.
Now the things of which we're talking we are mighty
 sure about—
So what's the use to strike the way you can't win out?

CHORUS

Tie 'em up! tie 'em up; that's the way to win.
Don't notify the bosses till hostilities begin.
Don't furnish chance for gunmen, scabs and all their
 like;
What you need is One Big Union and the One Big
 Strike.

II

Why do you make agreements that divide you when you
 fight,
And let the bosses bluff you with the contract's "sacred
 right,"
Why stay at work when other crafts are battling with
 the foe,
You must stick together don't you know.

The day when you begin to see the classes waging war
You can join in the biggest tie-up that was ever known
      before.
When the strikes all o'er the country are united into one
Then the workers One Big Union all the wheels shall run.

JOE HILL'S LAST WILL

(Written in his cell, November 18, 1915, on the eve of
his execution.)

My will is easy to decide,
For there is nothing to divide.
My kin don't need to fuss and moan—
"Moss does not cling to a rolling stone."
My body? Ah, if I could choose,
I would to ashes it reduce,
And let the merry breezes blow
My dust to where some flowers grow.
Perhaps some fading flower then
Would come to life and bloom again.
This is my last and final will.
Good luck to all of you,

                    JOE HILL.

Why should any worker be without the necessities of
life when ten men can produce enough for a hundred?

Why does a short work day and a long pay always go
together?

THE MYSTERIES OF A HOBO'S LIFE

(Air: "The Girl I Left Behind Me")

I took a job on an extra gang,
  Way up in the mountain,
I paid my fee and the shark shipped me
  And the ties I soon was counting.

The boss he put me driving spikes
  And the sweat was enough to blind me,
He didn't seem to like my pace,
  So I left the job behind me.

II

I grabbed a hold of an old freight train
  And around the country traveled,
The mysteries of a hobo's life
  To me were soon unraveled.

I traveled east and I traveled west
  And the "shacks" could never find me,
Next morning I was miles away
  From the job I left behind me.

III

I ran across a bunch of "stiffs"
  Who were known as Industrial Workers,
They taught me how to be a man—
  And how to fight the shirkers.

I kicked right in and joined the bunch
  And now in the ranks you'll find me.
Hurrah for the cause—To hell with the boss!
  And the job I left behind me.

WORKERS' MEMORIAL SONG

(Air: Russian Funeral March-Pochoronii Marsh)

Dying as soldiers fighting for Labor, so did you fall;
An off'ring of your love for those who share the strife;
Gladly you gave us talent and treasure; yielding your all.
The honor of the world, your freedom and your life.
Deeply you suffered nor shrunk from the grave—
Judges and hangmen, the fate of the fray;
Starved in dark dungeons, beaten and tortured—cheerful
    and brave —
Defying chains and jails, you marched upon your way.
Mad with their blood-lust, rich from our labor, exploiters
    dwell
In luxury and splendor; scornful of our power
Sweeping to triumph trusting no promise—Heaven or Hell;
This song of sorrow sounds to them their fatal hour.
Rise now ye workers rebellious and bold;
Tyrants no longer shall rule from above;
We are the builders—no one shall suffer hunger and
    cold —
We bring a world of beauty, liberty and love.
Farewell, true comrades, death now enfolds you—rest in
    the tomb;
As sleeping there in peace you know no more of pain.
Farewell, true comrades, we will remember you and your
    doom,
And labor soon will prove that none have died in vain.
Farewell, true comrades, we rise to the fight;
O'er-sweeping all 'neath the banner ye bore,
Slavery and sorrow vanish before us. Toilers, Unite!
To break your bonds and rule the world for evermore.
    (Repeat the last four lines of the last stanza.)

FAREWELL, FRANK!

(Air: "Barcarolle" from the "Tales of Hoffman")
By Gerald J. Lively

You've fought your fight, a long good night
   Is all that we can say.
Sleep on, sleep on, your work is done
   Brave fighter for the Day.
Kind Mother Earth who gave you birth
   Receives you to her breast.
For us the Fight, for you the night,
   The night of well earned rest,
No more you'll feel the cling of steel,
   You've burst the prison bars,
You gave your life in this our strife,
   Brave conqueror of stars.
Sleep on, sleep on, your work is done,
   Sleep on, sleep on, sleep on.

THE COMMONWEALTH OF TOIL

(Air: "Nellie Grey")

By Ralph Chaplin

In the gloom of mighty cities
  Mid the roar of whirling wheels,
We are toiling on like chattel slaves of old,
  And our masters hope to keep us
Ever thus beneath their heels,
  And to coin our very life blood into gold.

CHORUS

But we have a glowing dream
  Of how fair the world will seem
When each man can live his life secure and free.
  When the earth is owned by Labor
And there's joy and peace for all
  In the commonwealth of Toil that is to be.

II

They would keep us cowed and beaten
  Cringing meekly at their feet.
They would stand between each worker and his bread.
  Shall we yield our lives up to them
For the bitter crust we eat?
  Shall we only hope for heaven when we're dead?

III

They have laid our lives out for us
  To the utter end of time.
Shall we stagger on beneath their heavy load?
  Shall we let them live forever
In their gilded halls of crime
  With our children doomed to toil beneath their goad?

IV

When our cause is all triumphant
  And we claim our Mother Earth,
And the nightmare of the present fades away.
  We shall live with Love and Laughter,
We, who now are little worth,
  And we'll not regret the price we have to pay.

A WORKER'S PLEA

(Air: "Tuck Me to Sleep")

By T-B-S.

Old Kentucky cradled me—when I was young,
Then Ohio hired me—I sure got stung,
Night and day I've labored since—
Shucking corn and filling bins
And now, they say, my long, long rest begins.

CHORUS

'Tuck me to sleep in my old 'tucky home,
Cover me with roses, gravel, anything but stone,
Then let the dew drop a tear on my grave
Like a token never spoken to a broken-hearted slave—
I ain't had a bit of rest—masters thought it wasn't best;
—Thought that I could rest the best—afer I "go west."
'Tuck me to bed in my old 'tucky home,
Let me lay there—stay there, cover me up with loam.

II

Old Kentucky cradled me—'tis even true—
Since I came to IOWAY, she worked me too,
Every state in all this land
Used me for a hired hand,
But why I'm broke—I fail to understand.

III

Migratory working man, I'm on my way—
I am done with sun and sand and new-mown hay;
I have worked from sun to sun,
Nothing have I ever won
And now, thank God, my harvesting is done.

ORGANIZE!

(Tune: "The Green Fields of Dunmoor")
By James J. Ferriter

Come all you exploited workingmen
    And fight for Freedom's cause,
For you are bound, both hand and foot,
    By capitalistic laws;
Your voices you can raise no more,
    Your lips you now must seal,
For if you rise to speak a word
    A gun-man's at your heel.

Come on, unite, my hearty boys,
    And fight the common foe;
The rustling card with all its faults
    This time must surely go.
The "seven days" and "safety first,"
    Alas, they are no more,
So now's your time to fall in line
    At Freedom's onward roll.

Our master is a "patriot" true,
  Red wealth he has galore,
And all good things that Labor brings,
  He's locked up in his store;
But if, like men, you'll organize,
  His reign will be no more,
And he will go where he belongs
  A-shoveling copper ore.

Remember, then, the six-hour day
  Must be our first demand;
For miners from our ranks each day
  From death receive a call;
The miner's "con" you soon will see
  Will lose its deadly pall,
And we'll make this camp a grand old spot
  For the workers, one and all.

THERE IS POWER IN A UNION

By Joe Hill

(Tune: "There Is Power in the Blood")

Would you have freedom from wage slavery,
  Then join in the grand Industrial band;
Would you from mis'ry and hunger be free,
  Then come! Do your share, like a man.

CHORUS
There is pow'r, there is pow'r
In a band of workingmen,
When they stand hand in hand,
That's a pow'r, that's a pow'r
That must rule in every land—
One Industrial Union Grand.

Would you have mansions of gold in the sky,
  And live in a shack, way in the back?
Would you have wings up in heaven to fly,
  And starve here with rags on your back?

If you've had "nuff" of "the blood of the lamb"
  Then join in the grand Industrial band;
If, for a change, you would have eggs and ham,
  Then come, do your share, like a man.

If you like sluggers to beat off your head,
  Then don't organize, all unions despise,
If you want nothing before you are dead,
  Shake hands with your boss and look wise.

Come, all ye workers, from every land,
  Come, join in the grand Industrial band,
Then we our share of this earth shall demand.
  Come on! Do your share, like a man.

HARVEST LAND

(Air: "Beulah Land")

By T-D and H.

The harvest drive is on again,
John Farmer needs a lot of men;
To work beneath the Kansas heat
And shock and stack and thresh his wheat

CHORUS

Oh Farmer John—Poor Farmer John,
Our faith in you is over-drawn. ......
—Old fossil of the Feudal Age,
Your only creed is Going Wage—
"Bull Durham" will not buy our Brawn—
You're out of luck—poor farmer, Jawn.

You advertise, in Omaha,
"Come, leave the Valley of the Kaw."
Nebraska calls, "Don't be misled."
"We'll furnish you a feather bed!"

Then South Dakota "lets a roar,"
"We need ten thousand men—or more";
Our grain is turning—prices drop!
For God's sake save our bumper crop."

In North Dakota—(I'll be darn)
The "wise guy" sleeps in "hoosier's" barn
—Then hoosier breaks into his snore
And yells, "It's quarter after four."

CHORUS

Oh Harvest Land—Sweet Burning Sand!
—As on the sun-kissed field I stand
I look away across the plain
And wonder if it's going to rain—
I vow, by all the Brands of Cain,
That I will not be here again.

HOLD THE FORT

(English Transport Workers' Strike Song)

We meet today in Freedom's cause,
　And raise our voices high;
We'll join our hands in union strong,
　To battle or to die.

CHORUS

Hold the fort for we are coming—
　Union men, be strong.
Side by side we battle onward,
　Victory will come.

Look my Comrades, see the union
　Banners waving high.
Reinforcements now appearing,
　Victory is nigh.

See our numbers still increasing;
　Hear the bugles blow.
By our union we shall triumph
　Over every foe.

Fierce and long the battle rages,
　But we will not fear.
Help will come whene'er it's needed,
　Cheer, my Comrades, cheer.

WORKINGMEN, UNITE!

By E. S. Nelson

(Tune: "Red Wing")

Conditions they are bad,
And some of you are sad;
You cannot see your enemy,
The class that lives in luxury,—
You workingmen are poor,—
Will be for evermore,—
As long as you permit the few
To guide your destiny.

CHORUS

Shall we still be slaves and work for wages?
It is outrageous—has been for ages;
This earth by right belongs to toilers,
And not to spoilers of liberty.

The master class is small,
But they have lots of "gall."
When we unite to gain our right,
If they resist we'll use our might;
There is no middle ground,
This fight must be one round.
To victory, for liberty,
Our class is marching on!

Workingmen, unite!
We must put up a fight,
To make us free from slavery
And capitalistic tyranny;
This fight is not in vain,
We've got a world to gain.
Will you be a fool, a capitalist tool,
And serve your enemy?